Maybe I'm Supposed To Give You Advice

NATE BRANTINGHAM

Seattle Small Books Company
Seattle, WA

Seattle Small Books Company
Seattle, WA

First Edition

Maybe I'm Supposed To Give You Advice

Special thanks to Richard Neidhardt for his generous support.

"The Carpenter-Poet" first appeared in
The Monarch Review, 2016

Cover Design by
Lynn Walters

ISBN 978-0-9771575-3-2

Dedicated to my Dad
and to the Spokane poetry community

TABLE OF CONTENTS

Introduction

Poems for this book were originally written as spoken word pieces. They have each been performed at open mics and many of them at poetry slams. Converting them from spoken word to something that also works as written word was a real challenge. Luckily, my father is a written word poet and has offered guidance. With his help and the insightful editing provided by Dennis Held, this book came into being.

This would be a good place to point out that I tend to write about memories and emotions as they feel not as they were. I've exaggerated or outright lied and in some cases did even worse: I told the truth. There is no rhyme or reason to what or about whom I write beyond the feelings I try to convey. Some of the most important people in my life have no poems written about them (like my twin brother) and one person I barely know has three.

Nick Cave (who has one written about him) has said: "I feel like a cannibal, always looking for someone to cook in a pot." I've cooked a lot of people for my poems. I don't know if I should apologize more to those I decided to cook, or those who didn't end up in the pot. Either way, my sincerest hope is that these poems find meaning for you.

Galaxies and Hearts

They said that we were made of stardust
and like our ancestors who forged us,
we are slaves to each other's gravity.

There are galaxies within our hearts,
clots of dust given purpose
and ancient memories.

Why did you think this would be a gentle thing?
Celestial bodies do not kiss,
they crash.
Our love is measured by the impact craters.
And then we spin off again into the void.

But we are not pool balls
to leave no mark
as some hustler
racks and breaks us,
losing over and over,
until the stakes are high enough.

Nor are we bumper cars,
to bounce off one another
careening from person to person,
with nothing but a laugh
and some light whiplash.

Nor are we feathers
with a pull so light that
we all fall into each other
with a touch as soft
goose down.

No, for us,
every crash leaves its mark.
Consider the moon,
a child of collision,
one parent long gone.

The fire and heat of our creation
will be our undoing.

I do not say this to make excuses,
but to say I'm sorry.

I did not mean to come so close
to an event horizon I couldn't see
but could feel in every star-forged atom,
that moment of no turning back
when our touches felt like ground zero.

I'd leave a crater you would have to fill
with the lava in your heart.
That ancient dust,
repurposed again.

They say we are made of dead stars.
Nothing we ever do is gentle.

All These Pretty Words

What I mean to say Dad
is that I read your poem again
and I have no idea what you're saying.

You use these antiquated architecture terms
like "entablature" which was lost on me,
although I appreciated learning in the appendix
that an entablature is "the upper part of an order,
consisting of architrave, frieze and cornice."

But to be honest, I still don't know what an architrave is,
so you may want to define that somewhere
in the attached seven pages of appendix.

What I mean to say Dad
is that I missed the Ezra Pound references,
all the TS Elliot references,
and if I got the Beach reference
it was only because you capitalized "Beach"
although the word "caryatidinal" in the same line,
isn't even recognized by my spell check.
And yeah, I recognized the Latin words as Latin,
but I did not recognize them in a way
that correlates to understanding.

What I mean to say Dad
is that you'd need a few more degrees not dealing
with computers and business to understand this,
I don't have a background in comparative ancient literature
and a lifetime's worth of experience in construction,
and why didn't you ever remarry?

I'm sorry...

What I mean to say Dad
is that I heard from mom about her throwing plates at you,
and how you'd just sweep it all up.
And how one day she realized the only one

3

who missed the plates she had broken
was her.

And I guess that's what you look for.
Those moments when it's not worth the plate anymore,
or when the jokes about breaking up aren't funny anymore,
and when she doesn't ask if you want to
come with her on errands anymore.

What I mean to say Dad,
is that you always say the two of us,
my brother and myself,
are the best things
that ever came out of that marriage.

And I get that,
because when I look back and think back about my first wife
I know the best thing that ever came of that
was that I introduced her to the love of her life, her wife,
and the mother of her two beautiful daughters.

What I mean to say Dad
is that these old scars fade in time
and it doesn't even ache anymore
when the weather changes.

What I mean to say Dad
is that I'm sorry for introducing you
to another woman who wouldn't stick around.
And I know you loved her like your own,
because her name is on the inside
of your first book right next to mine.
A mistake caught in time.

And then another relationship failed
and this time it was my fault,
and the bedroom just next to my office,
that was supposed to be yours some day;
she told me so,
because that's what family does,

it takes care of each other.
It plans for things like failing health,
or unexpected children.
Until the family also fails,
and we didn't plan for that.
And I know you didn't either.

What I mean to say Dad,
is that I remember your story about playing a game of chess
as an amateur on a whim against a ranked master
and when you won you decided there wasn't any reason
to play chess anymore, and you never played again.
"Why bother?" you said, "I'll never do any better."

Maybe we aren't so different,
You didn't teach me how to build a house,
or the classics or poetry,
but I can sure build a wall
and hide behind all my words.

Small Mining

It's the day after a party.
One that I didn't actually attend.
I've got a small hammer in my hand
and I'm chipping away at a cinder block.

If it breaks free
I can open the way under this porch
where there's an engagement ring somewhere
dropped during the revelry the night before.

I am determined to find this ring
because they want me to
and it seems the only way left
for me to earn their friendship.

I wiggle under the porch
searching through mud and spiders
unearthing worms
but it is small mining.

I stay down there anyway.
I feel less out of place among the insects
than among the people I am here to meet.
So I keep looking in silence.

I can never know what would have happened
if I would have stayed at the party.
But there is no healing for the passing days
which die like canaries long forgotten.

The bold parts of me
want to die with my hands still
knuckle-white around the pickax.
Not here, under the porch.

Above me I hear the footsteps and
the idle conversations of a slow recovery.
For them the world slowly awakens,
but the ring was never found.

Murakami's Tangled Strings

The smell of her sweat and hair,
the feel of her head on my shoulder.
These things I'll never forget
even as her cries of pleasure still ringing in my ears
become more muted with every echo.

When I die I want to break time.
I want to watch this scene
over and over and over
and never the ones
that follow.

See, there's this moment when she looks
right into my eyes and I into hers.
In hers I see confusion
and in mine she sees the shame
of Murakami's tangled strings.

"What's wrong?" she asks.
It's a conversation I've been dreading.
I shake my head.
The words are too elusive,
I don't even know where to start.

"What's wrong?" she asks again.
Nothing is wrong with the moment.
Nothing is wrong with the woman.
Nothing is wrong with the pleasure I feel.
Nothing is wrong with this, just with me.

"I'm tired." I lie.
I lie into the shame,
a lie I want to believe,
a lie to cover the unspeakable truth,
a lie to delay the inevitable.

Her hand is resting on my naked stomach
her breath cooling against the sweat on my skin,

echoing the cooling in her heart.
The slow pulling away I've come to expect,
the moment I've never grown used to.

But this moment gives way to the next,
passion diffuses to excuses,
her eyes flicker nervously around the room
and I know that in all but name,
I have lost this woman.

And this after I had told myself
that I would never again open this door
to my own undoing.
It is the bravest of talks.
And then I looked at her face.

Music has been my crutch.
It speaks to me in a language
I myself cannot pronounce.
"For once" sings Jason,
"I almost was good enough."

And I think of Alina Simone,
singing the songs of a dying country,
the inevitability of disappointment and disillusionment,
the death of all good sweet dreams
blinking slowly, cold and dead above us.

And if you hear me humming
in these moments of shame
it is only because my own voice adds nothing
to those who have sung their own
cold and broken Hallelujahs.

Nevada rocks

If you keep following the 195 South
you will find a stretch of Nevada highway
with salt flats pressed against both sides
and distant mirages which really may be water.
I couldn't tell.

The speed limit here is 80 and cars
rush past this chalk-white plain

Small rocks, the size of fists
rest dark on the desert
where people have gathered them
in the ancient language of love and math
spelling out two names
added together by basalt.

The rocks will stand the sun,
will last the brief rains
and the howling wind,
and still spell the lovers' names.
Giving some illusion of permanence
and a way to leave our mark
on a transient world.

Other travelers stop
to add their names
and prove their love as well
but these rocks are scarce
and so are taken from other claims
which in turn are picked apart,
love undone to spell new names,
and express other loves,

the most accurate analogy for love I know.

What's It Called?

Do you ever feel like maybe you missed
some critical stage in development?
Where you learn the names for your feelings
and how to express them?
Like Helen Keller and the water,
you have felt this over and over
but you never knew it had a name.

What's that emotion?
That one that creeps up on you at a house party,
pressed close to a hundred of your closest strangers
the smell of beer, sweat and tobacco filling the room.
She smiles at you from beneath her lavender hair
and pierces your gaze with her dark, dark eyes.
She is radiant.

But then your phone buzzes with a message:
"I guess you can stop by since you're in town."
And now your phone is a fiery brick burning your palm
with a promise that maybe this time you won't mess it up.
So you leave the warm sure-fire moment
for the cold, damp, Olympia night air,
and the chance to put things right.

She is a forty-five minute walk away.
You've never seen this place in the daylight,
have never walked this road
or turned right at the only streetlight for miles
to travel this empty highway at midnight.
Your shoes slap against the wet pavement
that you suspect has never been dry.

What's that emotion?
The one you feel when you look back the way you came
and that other one, maybe the same one,
that makes you sling your overnight pack
over your shoulder and secure it in place
in a fit of wild optimism and commit
to the most lost of all causes

There is no moon,
there are no lights,
there are no cars,
just you, an impossibly dark highway,
and the damp forest mildewing against you
a presence you smell and feel more than see in the night.
This emotion is called fear, I know this one.

She is like this forest.
She is cold and damp against your heart
and she reminds you of this dark empty road
and the way the trees blot out the stars.
The optimist in you keeps trying to look
for a light that isn't there,
headlights that aren't approaching.

You are keenly aware you have left the safe behind
for a taste of mystery
and a long sought swig of redemption.
If this fails, you will have proven yourself a fool
and will walk back cold and alone
once more through this forest
with no lavender hair to greet you this time.

"That was a long walk" she says.
And you shrug because nothing you can do or say
then or now
can explain the way that walk felt
or the thoughts that bounced in your head
These feelings that you cannot put a name to.
What's it called?

The one you feel when she hugs you?
What's it called?
The one you feel when she invites you in.
What's it called?
The one you feel when she presses her body against you in bed.
What's it called?
The one you feel when you look into her eyes.

What's it called?
The one you feel when she says after,
"I wasn't sure until I tried,
but I...
I feel *nothing.*"

Tombstones

This room is filled with future tombstones
which throw back an echo
that I have needed to hear
my whole life.

But it's coming from every direction
and it's tangled in on itself.
I believe in the future
but I don't trust it.

I don't trust you either,
but that's on me.
Everything you've ever said
was laced with integrity,

but these echoes
make me wonder,
and your honesty
sounds like arsenic.

But that's on me.
So just heap it on top
one burden at a time
I can take it.

I am sick of being lonely
and will take the abrasive contact
of your straw burdens
against my skin over another night alone.

I have a lifetime of practice
so pile it high
until my camel-back breaks
and my spine straightens.

Maybe then I can stand up taller
look you in the eyes
and give up on being the shortest
person in the room.

We are who we were at fourteen.
I don't believe I have grown an inch
although I've left 4 foot 8 long ago.
It's just the way our minds work.

How I can look down at your eyes
from an even six feet
and still feel like I'm looking up
because "time trumps distance."

I told her that with text and voice
but never in person
because distance has always won
every battle we never had.

We are all in a losing war
with our own minds
our own bodies
and our perceptions.

Put fat on her thighs
and they'll call her ugly,
put fat in her tits
and they'll call her sexy.

I didn't make the rules,
but there comes a time
when people stopped telling us
about ugly ducklings and swans.

These stories gave us hope when we were younger.
Now their silence conveys the belief
that sometimes the ugly ducklings
just become ugly ducks.

As if looks
were any measure of a person.
Just because I recognize the symptoms
doesn't mean I'm not guilty.

So I've ground up my own tombstone
and use it for cat litter.
You can smell the dust in my empty house
over the putrid stench of boredom.

Take this straw off my back
one twig at a time now
and make something beautiful
out of our burdens.

Everything you do
is beautiful,
you who walk with
epitaphs carved in your souls.

I'll win against neither time nor space
so bury me now beneath the shroud
you made from my straw
and don't forget to bring matches.

We have a fire to start tonight
and a city to burn,
so let's start with our hearts
and go from there.

The only makeup you'll need are ashes
the only pencil is charcoal
the light is a cinder
and none of us will ever be lonely again.

Nelson

3:30 PM
I'm in Nelson, BC
and it's so cold dreams freeze
before they hit the ground.
And shatter into a thousand half-hopes
Useless and derivative
Like this trip up here.
Like thinking this would help.

5:30 PM
I duck into the library which
shares a building with the police department.
I wonder how many people in Nelson
end up in both places on the same night.
I sit down for a while because it's warm
and open until 8 on weekdays.
The girl behind the desk is gorgeous.

6:30 PM
My phone is off to avoid the international rates
and I stare at it and hate its silence.
Murakami is telling me a story,
if I could just focus on his words.
Book, phone, girl,
my eyes spend equal measure on each
and I feel the restlessness of the hunted.

8:15 PM
The concert is packed,
and Becky is screaming into the microphone.
The guitar washes over her vocals,
washes over my sins.
Print me out and tear me up
and sprinkle me over this audience
like so many restraining orders.

3:00 AM
I'm looking for the border crossing that's still open
and driving between them over mountain passes.
It's single digits cold outside,
and they sprayed chemicals to turn the ice to slush.
My doctor wants me to try the same.
A new chemical for every problem except which border is open.
It's Patterson, by the way.

3:15 AM
Coming to Canada didn't fix my problems
and even in sport mode I can't outrun them,
the pedal down and all six cylinders screaming.
Maybe if I had a faster car or traveled further I could be free,
but maybe they don't make a car fast enough for loneliness.
"Wait," says a voice, "But they do!
It's that chemical truck up ahead, and it is coming your way."

Washing Machine

There's a video of these guys
who put a brick in a front load washer
and tell it to do the only thing it knows how.
It starts to quiver and shake
like a white lie
but it spins.

You should have been there to see it!
The way it shook and rattled
pulling its bolts out
spinning off the dials
door ripping off
and still it spins,
breaking the mounts
breaking off the fittings.
And it spins.
It just keeps spinning.
And at some point it stops being funny.

I'm no longer rooting for the brick,
although I've known plenty in my life.
It's the machine I'm cheering for.

Before long it is flying around the place
glorious and angry
like a junkyard dog on a leash.
But it keeps doing the only thing it knows how
this one trick pony at the end of its life
sitting on a pallet in the junkyard
which may as well be the glue factory
throwing off its shell
throwing off the dials
throwing off the bolts and screws and mounts
flinging the ring across the room,
shouting words it can't take back,
and it spins,
throwing parts of itself to the plains of Iowa
with her wife and children, and it spins,

bits flying across town where the enchiladas
are made by hand
and it spins
to unheard punk rock music, it spins.
Dancing steps it doesn't know, it spins.

And it's sorry.
This is just all it knows how to do.
With the dials missing,
every cycle looks the same,
no matter what you call them,
no matter what her name was.

Everything looks the same once it's gone,
and we all die alone-

Scrap in a junkyard.

But *damn* it gave it everything it had
and if it now rusts in a thousand pieces
spread out over three counties
well, at least it saw it through to the end
and you can't fault it for that.
You can't fault it for that.

Goodbye

My friend has a nervous disease she doesn't like to talk about.
At home at night she checks herself for injuries before bed
to see if anything happened in the day that she didn't feel
and by the same measure,
I have a dating profile.

But don't look for me here,
I'm using OK Cupid to travel Europe-
and Prague is beautiful this time of year.
Witty, charming, and with careful camera angles
my profile is everything I am not, and everywhere I wish I could
be.

It's easier from a distance
to dull the sting of failure and
to remove yourself from hope.
At home optimism means changing my sheets.
At a few thousand miles,
it just means getting dressed in the morning.

At two thousand miles
I get four pictures of my friend's naked chest.
"Which makes me look best?" she asks.
And I saw out my heart
and bury my dreams
and say "2nd from the bottom, she'll like that."
And I'm right, because taste I have.
It's courage I don't.

I'm leaning against the wall now,
as far removed from the crowd as I can get.
Places like this overwhelm me with a mixture
of envy and disappointment.
Sometimes you can feel most alone in a crowd
when it reminds you just how much you don't belong.

I stand just outside a small group of acquaintances.
But that's only so I don't look like I'm alone.

I say nothing and my eyes keep roving.
I'm getting jittery now.
There's a restlessness in me I cannot describe
but if I had its true name I could finally cast the spell
to free me from its yoke.
There's power in names they say,
but I don't know who said that.
I'm not very good with names.

The restlessness is mounting
as my eyes keep scanning the crowd.
Any hope I've had on arriving
has evaporated one failure at a time.
And I realize I am invisible
so I slide through the walls
with a backwards glance
to cast my own spell using
fire, gasoline, and speed.

If it seems like I am driving too fast
down these nighttime city streets
it's only because I'm still and always running
from these feelings just behind me
that I cannot put a name to.

Let's just call this one
"goodbye."

The Carpenter-Poet

His hands are huge-
tools and boards,
sheetrock and girders
have roughed his hands with thick calluses.

He has built houses
and refurbished stores.
Half of Pike Place Market
has seen his hands on the walls.

Before it opens, he knocks on a roll-up door,
muffling the smells of a bakery.
The door opens barely a foot
and a cinnamon roll appears.

This man will return the next day
as he has always done.
Again he is told to come back tomorrow
and the cycle continues.

But those too-thick hands,
I know they hold books during lunch break,
some written in Latin,
some in Greek.

And here's the secret of Pike Place.
Behind the walls and floorboards
you can find drafts of poems and translations
scratched into the studs or backing boards.

Go look yourself:
find the Catullus translated behind the sink
of that little Asian restaurant
next to the new drain pipe.

Go find the comments about Sisyphus
there behind the wall overlooking the Sound
where container ships load and unload,
load and unload.

Poetry behind the mirrors,
poetry on two-by-fours,
poetry under bathroom tiles,
poetry behind the sewer lines.

Thousands of feet stepping,
without knowing,
over the poetry written
just under the surface.

Because that is where poetry lives.

His hands are huge-
This carpenter-poet
who writes all his best works
with a carpenter's pencil.

If you want to know who he is,
look for the worker
whose belt is full of tools
required for the two trades.

Look for the one who does geometry
like he's read the original text,
the one who speaks
like he knows where words come from.

Look for the poet
with chalk and graphite
clinging to his fingers,
sticky with cinnamon rolls.

Look for the carpenter with
a book in his lunchbox.
The one conjugating verbs
to the rhythm of his hammer.

You may not find him
but his words still remain,
where the carpenter-poet
placed them just under the surface.

Because that is where poetry lives.

Sand Castles

When I was a child, I was playing on the beach
and I set my shovel close to the waves.
By the time I noticed, the waves had carried it out
beyond my feeble means

I woke my parents who were napping in the shade
to which they said it was too far out already
and turned it into a lesson on neglect
and of consequences.

I was assured there would be other shovels
but how does a future of other beaches
help a child who has castles and dreams to build
on this beach, on this day?

I'm paddling at the shore
to try to pull the blue shovel back
while I watch the waves bring it up into view
and then out again.

There *were* other shovels and other beaches
but of that shovel,
one time a wave lifted it up for me to see,
and then never again.

I told myself that when I was an adult
I would never say, "It's too far gone to try"
and now I am an adult
who has said this thing.

Waiting for the tide turn.

Ancient Gods

There was a time
when the merciless cold of night
and the inescapable press of nature
demanded fear.

And from fear came reverence
and from reverence came worship
where there was no pretense of justice,
no aura of righteousness.

Our early gods were ruthless
as was the hunger of those things
which moved in the night
and stole away our lives.

Early Gaia would pull you to her bosom,
cradle you against her breast
and whisper in your ear,
"I'm hungry."

We built walls.
Walls of leather,
walls of wood,
walls of brick.

We built cities and temples
philosophies and math
with no room for gods
to slip between the perfect angles.

We stood back an admired our growing culture,
our taming of the world.
Our conquering of nature.
Our internal divinity.

We broke the gods like horses.
Tied them to our plows where
they exist only to serve us,
tethered beside nature herself.

Today we don't need gods.
We don't fear the weather
or give much thought to disease
or famine.

Within our perfect walls,
we are impervious to the outside world.
Untouchable.
Unbreakable.

We have won.
Good game, nature.
We have nothing left to fear
but ourselves now.

"So do me a favor,"
says Gaia before she must concede.
"Stretch your feeble arms out
as wide as they will go.

If your stretched wide arms
represented the timeline of this one
insignificant planet
over which you crawl like maggots,

all of human history
from the cavemen to now
could be removed
with a nail file.

You will soon join your place,
not amongst the gods,
but amongst
the dinosaurs.

Consider your life now
as nothing more than
fingernail dust
about to settle on the cold tile floor

that was never yours
to begin with."

Squirrel

There's a squirrel beneath the house,
so I set a trap, loaded with peanuts.
It's a live trap, because I'm a pacifist
and violence and death never solved anything.
They just push the guilt around the table like poker chips.

I check it every day but it never catches the squirrel.
I hear it down there at night, chewing on pipes
or insulation,
or discarded memories.
I check the trap every day.

Until I forget.

I have to take its body out of the trap
using a twig to pry its locked jaws
off the bars
and peel its paws off of the cage.
I don't know why it didn't just give up
and go die in the corner like it was supposed to.

But this cage was made too well;
my memory made too poor.

Every clock that ever ticked,
ticks for you.
Every second that ever passed,
passes for you.

I've been the captor,
but I've also been the squirrel
trapped and doomed.

In the maternity ward
a song is played for every birth.
There is no song for giving up,
just that long, high whine
two stories up,
and a nurse with his fingers on a wrist
devoid of pulse.

Giving up is supposed to look like
Doritos and cats, lots of cats.
But it doesn't.
It looks like a dollar bill left on a table
next to a glass of water.
I slink out so as not to have to explain
to the waitress that my date never showed.
I've said to this waitress twice already
"I'll order in a minute, I'm still waiting for one more."
Before I leave without my dignity,
which is still at the bar, drinking.
It's the second time this week.
My dignity orders a double
while I drive home fast and reckless.

Giving up looks like the ace bandage
left in Tracy's medicine cabinet.
There are no bras in the house to replace it,
so she, she's a she today,
goes out without.
HRT is just so expensive,
and dignity just so cheap.

There's a boy on the junior high
basketball court,
who reminds me of myself.
He isn't watching the ball anymore.
He's just watching the clock,
waiting for it to run out
so he can just go home.

But then there's also this squirrel under my house
trapped in a metal rectangle
of almost the same proportions
as the metal rectangle I live in above it.
Its teeth are still on the bars,
and it will die soon,
alone,
still pulling,
still pulling.

Like Sands Through the Hourglass

"Like sands through the hourglass
So are the days of our lives."

And in the first few seconds of that iconic introduction
to the soap opera "Days of our Lives"
we can see only a growing pile of sand,
and a trickle coming from the top of the hourglass
with no indication of how many grains remain.

And this, to me, is the most terrifying thing of all.
That above us sits a finite number of days,
and all we can do is watch them pile up around us.

The translation of this introduction is roughly:
YOLO or Carpe Diem
depending on your age.

The introduction lasts for exactly 30 seconds.
There are 12,765 episodes.
Which means that an avid viewer
has seen 12,765 daily affirmations to do something with their life.
Watching those 12,765 half-minute introductions
back to back
would take four and a half days.

There are roughly 250 episodes a year.
Which translates to 250 hours a year,
or just under 10 and a half days of straight viewing, a year.
To be reminded daily,
that "like sands through the hourglass
so are the days of our lives."

To watch every episode would take an investment of
11,515 hours or 480 days straight.
Assuming you could watch them,
without sleeping.
During the course of this viewing,
329 new episodes will have aired.

Extrapolate that out to the nation,
just domestically,
and based on Nielson statistics,
an excel sheet
and too much time on my hands,
I have calculated that
the American public has invested
235.2 million hours into this show.
Or roughly 26,850 person years.
Which, according to Dr. Heribert Illig and Franz Löhner,
is almost exactly how many people years,
and I mean almost *exactly*,
it took the ancients to build the great pyramid.

Far be it for me to decide which is the greater art,
I cannot fathom the making of the great pyramid
any more than I can the making of the late nineties
love pyramid between Carrie/Austin/Sami and Mike.
And no one will really know how the pyramids were made
just like we'll never know why when Tom came back from
The Korean war with amnesia it was his own sister Marie
that he fell so in love with.

I mean, I don't want to tell you what to do with your life,
but, "like sands through the hourglass
so are the days of our lives."
And one by one,
episode by episode,
they fall around our feet.
And we will never know how many we have left.
And we will never get any of them back.

Toilet Paper

When preparing for a party as a single guy,
always remember the essentials.
I know you have plenty of beer in the fridge
but did you remember what happens after?
Did you remember the toilet paper?

I know as a guy,
you don't always use that much
But women, and I hope there are women at your party,
will use it every darn time!

And some women don't just use a square or two
They will fold your 2 ply over on itself again and again until it's
a 64 ply sponge.
And you'll be glad you had someone remind you to be an adult
and buy the toilet paper ahead of the party.

And that's where I was.
I had the toilet paper, the vacuuming done.
I was kicking butt,
it was like 1950s Cleaver household at my place.
I'm folding laundry.
I have a laugh track going.

And then I get to the bottom of the laundry and there's a fitted
sheet.
How do you fold a fitted sheet?

You don't.

You bundle it up like your frustration and your rage
and you bury it in the back of your closet and hope you never
see it again.
And now it's a very different 1950s.

And that laugh track isn't laughing *with* you, it's laughing *at* you.
It's the real 1950s.
It's the, "I'll give you something to cry about" 1950s.

The "Real men don't cry" 1950s.
The "June, you get back in the kitchen this doesn't involve you"
1950s,
the one where the letters P T S and D don't mean anything when
put together 1950s.

They called it shell shocked back then.
But even then they had paid for the studies
to show that it was the sissies and the momma's boys,
the ones still tied to the apron strings who would come back
damaged from a war others had deemed just.
But it wasn't.
It was the ones who early and best had learned the lesson
thou shalt *NOT* kill
who had trouble with the killing.

And the dying.

But hey, 1950s was a great time for Spokane.
We had Bing Crosby and the railroads...

And we still have the railroads
and the way those brakes squeal
like dying boys and the box cars slam
together like machine gun fire
and my friend grabs my arm
and it's the first time he's touched me since he's been back.
I look in his eyes and it's not friendship I see-
It's fear.
And then shame.
And I would have thought we'd have
gotten past that by now.

This was supposed to be about parties and toilet paper.

But then, he was supposed to be a hero.

There's nothing I can do about it now,
but I have a couple cold beers in the fridge
so maybe let's just try to have a good time tonight.
Let's just try to have a good time.

A Dozen Points Of Sex Advice

1. Communicate. Talk about it with your partner. If you can't, you aren't mature enough yet. If your partner can't they aren't mature enough yet.

2. No still means no.

3. If you cannot laugh at the absurdity of sex, you're doing it wrong. There are a lot of elbows.
> a. Do not place anything on your headboard you do not want to come flying off of your headboard.
> b. This especially includes water.

4. Sex with men is like playing a video game on easy after entering the Konami code. If you still manage to lose at this point, blame the equipment, no one could win.
> a. Sex with women is like playing the game on hardcore with one life and if you lose the game itself destructs and kills you and sometimes it will be rude and tells all your other games how bad you are.
> b. Speaking of the Konami code, if in doubt, try that on anything you can get your fingers/tongue on.
> c. If you don't know the Konami code, it may be you aren't old enough to be having sex.
>> i. Or you're too old.
>>> 1. There is no such thing as too old.
>> ii. There *is* such a thing though as too young. Why are you in such a hurry?!

5. Pets will be very curious in what the commotion is all about and will also be very disappointed if you fail to make them puppies. Talk with them ahead of time and prepare them for the disappointment.
> a. You cannot make them puppies in this way.

6. If all else fails and you cannot find a partner, use the same technique the school system employs to keep kids passing: Lower your standards and include more technology.

7. Porn ends when the guy finishes, in real life, ain't nobody finishing anything until your partner get's theirs. Then it's negotiable, but be prepared for additional rounds.

8. When she says she wants to roleplay, she does not mean she wants you to be your D&D character in bed.
>   a. If she does mean this, give her my number, I'm a minotaur shaman.
>   b. To clarify, she usually doesn't mean she wants you to play a rogue and break down her back door to steal all her booty.
>>   i. Approach this topic with care and communicaion.
>   c. Speaking of magic you do not have a magic penis unless it was made in Japan and contains batteries, so put your rod of quickness in your sack of holding, young Galahad, this isn't about you.

9. If you find yourself in a situation with multiple partners, round robin works best.
>   a. Start with the one you are least attracted to, this will keep it interesting.
>>   i. Don't be disappointed when they want to start with you. I'm sure they just haven't read my list.

10. Everyone hates condoms.
>   a. So don't use one, you don't drink your beer with the cap still on do you?
>>   i. I'm kidding. Always use one.
>>>   1. But you don't have to like them.
>>   ii. reiterated for emphasis all kidding aside. Always use one.

11. Sex is like punk rock. There is no shortage of experience or skill that cannot be made up for by your enthusiasm and possibly some piercings.

12. Your partner is another broken human being lost in a world too cruel for love floundering and struggling just like you are. Treat your partners with care.

Speling

You've all seen those spelling and grammer memes:

"I don't judge people based on race, creed, color or gender.
I judge people based on spelling, grammar, punctuation and sentence structure."

"Spelling is difi... Chalen.... Spelling is hard."

"When I see incorrect spelling in a Facebook post, I feel compelled to
use the correctly spelled word in my comment. I'm helpful like that."

"You had me at your impeccable spelling and correct use of grammar."

These are the ways
we use education and ability
to make ourselves feel superier to the people around us.
We rale against your and you're as it it makes a like of difference,
because it's always easier to tear down than to build up.

Maybe I just got an ask to grind,
Maybe it's the 19% on the spelling section of the
national high school tests?
Maybe it's just being told over and over
that I can't spell worth a dam.
I don't know.
But I can tell you how libarati.... How freeing... it was to learn
that Chaucer spelled his own name
4 different ways, and that spelling and grammer
are both modern invitations used primarily to distinguish levels of education.

Every meme we post, like those I read before,
Shamming those who have trouble spelling,
Or learning disabilities,
Or frankly just different prioritys,

Doesn't set up as some sort of Internet supper user.
It just makes us another bully picking on the kids who weren't
good at sports.
"Hey Billy, you get this?
This kid doesn't know what a lateral pass is,
and sometimes on top of that,
this kid he uses incomplete sentences
with implied subjects.
What is this Billy? Is this amatur hour?"

Every time you correct someone's spelling you do two things:
Shame them.
Encourage them to lower there... The... Their standards.
Repeated corrections can be tied to students writing shorter
papers,
on safer subjects,
using smaller words.
If that's the goal, then by all means, rudely corect they're spelling.
Publicly when possible.

When I was scoring my 19%,
my friend was scoring so low
the statistics engine just gave up
and said he was an "outlier."
And not in a good way.
He'd given up,
the school system had given up,
and passed him just because they felt guilty holding him back
yet another year for a hopeless cause, and no collage would have
him.

It wasn't easy, reading his writing,
Trying to find meening in his seemingly random arrangement of
letters
He would never write again,
or read if he could help it except for one thing.

In 1998, we started to play Everquest,
And online game, with swords,
Magic,

1000s of online players
And a whole lot of typing.

He was the silent player,
Never saying anything in the group,
Not reading the franticaly typed instructions
To fall back,
Or heel this person,
Or target that enemy,
And the ridicule continued.
We just told the other players he was a bit of a lose cannon
But here, for the first time, was an insentive...
Reson to keep trying,
And as his character got levels,
So did he,
Eventually able to warn the noobs of a train to zone,
or zon at any rate.

He was learning to type past and around a disability,
He fought for every word that was close enough.
It will never be prefect.
But sometimes "close enough" represents
more of an achivement then we could ever know.

He's the most loyal friend I've ever known.
The one I call when things go to carp and I need a rescue.
He has never let me down.
But hey,
let's keep posting about how proper grammer and spelling
is what you look for first.
Remind him,
again,
that he's not good enough to be your freind.
Remind him
again
that his ideas have no value
because they don't conform to your presentation standards.

You just go ahead and do that.
We're too busy saving the noobs from a train to zon over here.

Maybe I'm Supposed To Give You Advice

Maybe I should tell you it gets better,
that losing at a young age taught me how to win later,
or at least be a better loser,
or go down gracefully,
or shake off a blow,

Because surely life isn't just a repeat of seventh grade
like how Steinbeck's East of Eden
was really just Cain and Abel
over and over again
told eight different ways in the same book.
Or that people won't keep saying,
"Don't worry, I think you're great,
I'm sure you'll get picked next time,"
handing out sincerity as a consolation prize
so often that you can't even taste it anymore.

Maybe I'm supposed to tell you
that you won't see your friends and colleagues
glide past you with barely an effort
while you're still chasing dreams that looks like clouds,
or clouds that look like dreams.
That they won't get huge houses,
fancy cars and beautiful families,
or land gigs,
or take perfect selfies every.damn.day.
That you won't feel a mix of pride and disappointment
at every friend's success
And that you won't feel guilty for this.
That you won't wonder why you weren't included,
and come to the only answer that fits:
you just weren't good enough.
How many "maybe next times" do you need
before you can be statistically sure
that it's not chance anymore?
And there is no next time.

Maybe I'm supposed to tell you
that the curse of feeling mediocre will end-
that dreadful limbo zone where you feel good enough to try
but not good enough to succeed-
so close your breath fogs against the glass ceiling.
Maybe I'm supposed to tell you that
You will not always feel
adjacent and auxiliary to real talent.
An after thought
if there's room in the program.

Maybe I'm supposed to tell you
that depression,
once beat,
won't come back.
But your lover will.

That soon every fight you regret will
cancel with every love you regret,
and when you blow away the dust,
confidence will be sitting like a nugget
in the palm of your hand,
re-writing the lines
so that any fortune teller will say,
"Now *this* is a life well blessed."

Maybe I'm supposed to tell you
that eventually every poem you write
becomes a love letter to yourself.
That there comes a time when you stop
sending emails to yourself,
just to make sure that your
acceptance didn't get lost in transit
or that your account is still active.

Maybe I'm supposed to tell you
that you won't lie awake at night
trying to recall the last moment
in your life when you felt purpose.
That eventually all will stand revealed,

glorious and beautiful and worth it.
SO incredibly worth it.
That somewhere in your life will come the pivot,
when you will shatter that glass ceiling
and never look back.

Maybe I'm supposed to tell you it's coming.

The Little Things

On May 23rd, 1998 she had drunk more coffee in 1 sitting than she ever had or would again in her life.

This was followed, almost immediately, by her 2nd longest pee (one minute and fourteen seconds before the first break in the stream, surpassed only by a time, almost exactly 2 years later, when she set about to prove that she could outdo her standing alcohol record set on her 21st birthday on this, her 22nd birthday. She failed in this endeavor, by 3 beers and 1 shot, but did manage to set the personal longest pee record.)

Her longest run on sentence spanned an impressive 186 words, written for an 11th grade English class on March 7th, 1995. This same paper had the most spelling errors per volume with an average of 3 per line, and 1.2 grammatical mistakes. This paper was written during what can only be described as her 3rd worst breakup experience. It would not have ranked so highly except for the early age of its occurrence which lent an air of teenage angst to the whole affair.

However, her longest parenthetical statement would come 3 years later, penned on October 21st, 1999 in an essay on Kierkegaard. Unsurprisingly, this also got the award for most parenthetical statement awards given on a single assignment with a whopping 7 students setting such records out of a class of 35. Only 22 would pass this class. This is not a record. That would come in Spring term 2000 when a perfect storm of bureaucracy would derail 18 students, including her, in a class of 26 before the second week.

July 2nd 2002 would go down as the day in which she would set a personal record for sex with the most partners in a 24 hour period (7), most orgasms in a 24 hour period (9) and most orgasms given in a 24 hour period (8), all during what would be another record for largest orgy of her life (it was supposed to be an adult toy party with an attendance of 10). This was coupled with most sexual partners whose names she didn't know (3), most sexual partners names she *did* know but then forgot (4), and was an event which spawned the most hours questioning her own sexuality (47 cumulative hours) the results of which was settled by an event on August 14 2002.

March 30th 2003 would be the worst car accident of her life and 4th closest she got to death without actually dying (surpassed by a heart attack in 2047, another in 2049 and a fall in 2056).

February 17th, 2004 was the moment she felt most in love with another human being, when her girlfriend at the time stopped traffic to try and catch an injured bird which had been left dazed and damaged by a passing car. The bird was delivered to a veterinary clinic, and they had their second most passionate lovemaking session that night, surpassed only by a random moment on December 29th 2006 when both of them were just "on" but that was a force-of-nature type experience and you just can't account for those. This relationship would turn out to be her second longest and the ending of it would take the record for biggest heartbreak, but again, some things you just can't account for.

She would wake up on June 7th 2005 wondering if her life was special (it was) if there was anything unique about her (there is), and if this day would be just like the rest (it wasn't). She would leave her house to go to work, just after a rain storm, and set two records in a single walk. One for getting hit with the most sprinklers that didn't need to be on (3 strikes in 18 blocks) and one for stepping over the most worms on a single walk. This would never be known to her, and so she would continue to worry, but it did matter to the worms. Her life mattered to someone else more times than it mattered to her at a ratio of 14.328:1. She would never learn how to see the little things that made each day special, just as she would never see the impact she made on the lives of those around her. But then, statistically speaking, very few ever do.

A Dream About Nick Cave

I had a dream about Nick Cave,
singer, songwriter, composer, author, poet.
The important thing about this dream
is that it was not, in fact, about Nick Cave.
No, it was about a fisherman in Alaska,
salt-haired and weathered skin.
See, he was a fan of Nick Cave's music,
and would play it on his boat.
While waves crashed,
Nick Cave would sing,
"Once there came a storm in the form of a girl,
and it blew to pieces my snug little world."

This Alaskan fisherman also had a dream,
to write a biography of Nick Cave
while traveling with him on his next world tour.
And so he sold everything he owned
and managed to talk Nick Cave into agreeing
to take him on the world tour
so he could write his book.
Because to Nick Cave,
"all the towers of ivory are crumbling,
and the swallows are sharpening their beaks"
which is Nick Cave for: "this sounds like fun."

However, it becomes evident that this isn't
about an Alaskan biographer at all.
No, it's about a filmmaker hired by Nick Cave
to make a film about this Alaskan fisherman turned biographer
as he travels with Nick Cave on his world tour.
In some "Exit Through the Giftshop" twist,
this filmmaker himself is now the center of the dream about
the fisherman and Nick Cave.
The three of them are having this talk,
documented on film,
and in salty notepads,
about the inherent unidirectional sharing
of experiences that comes with artistic expression,

be it music, writing, or film.

Everyone knows what Nick Cave's music *feels* like,
and by extension, a little about Nick Cave,
and yet Nick Cave knows nothing about those
who listen to his music.

And while Nick Cave was singing
"Come sail your ships around me,
and burn your bridges down"
it wasn't because he was aware of an
Alaskan fisherman who literally sailed ships around
and then figuratively burnt all his bridges down
to write a biography about Nick Cave.

The three of them bemoaned this sorry
state of cultural artistic expression,
And then BANG
I become aware
that I am *in* this dream,
perhaps even pivotal in it
as I am currently watching
what turns out to be the final cut of the filmmaker's film
about the filmmaker who is making a film
about a biographer who is taking notes
while on tour with a singer
who is himself
the one and only,
Nick Cave.

And it becomes my task
to change the history of unidirectional cultural expression
by impacting the movie
as it plays
and thus completing the loop
and prove that artistic expression can go both ways,
and using only the power of my mind
and the deep desire burning inside me
I watch awestruck as the Alaskan fisherman
scratches into his notepad,

in the pre-recorded movie,
"Go see Nate in Spokane."
thus proving art is bi-directional,
and maybe this *does* mean that
Nick Cave was aware
on some level,
of the fisherman when he sang,
"The sea will swallow up the mountains,
and the sky will throw thunderbolts and sparks,
straight at you."
But I don't know if Nick Cave will actually ever come to see me,
because of the disappointingly unidirectional nature
of dreaming.
But now every fisherman carries a promise
and every mackerel is a portent
whispering to me now in the fish isle
that Nick Cave is coming. He's coming.

Catfish

She says she'll send me a picture,
just as long as I don't dare use it
to catfish anyone.

But isn't imitation
the sincerest form of flattery?

I don't just want to *see* you,
I want to *be* you.

I want to take your digital skin
and wrap it around my body
until my grey hairs turn blonde,
my age fades into your youth,
and my failures melt into your infinite future.
Call it a study.

Call it watching how people treat me when I'm me
versus how they treat me when they think I'm you.
You call it a lie.
I call it science.
This isn't the first time
those two have been confused.

Like there is anyone who wouldn't take a pill
to be someone else for a while,
to try life in someone else's shoes.
After all, we read books and
go to movies and play video games.
Like a friend I once had who pretended to be
his dead girlfriend when he played games online,
to *be* her, since he couldn't be *with* her.
For a while, it was like they were together again,
playing games like they used to,
before the overdose.
Once we found out,
none of us blamed him
but none of us could quite treat him the same either.

And what happens when the body you slip into
feels more at home than the one you were born in,
and your digital dress-up turned fantasy,
turns bitter reality when you look into the mirror
and see only yourself looking back.
Now you'll need a lot better of a costume,
to keep all this self hatred away

Simple experiments can turn complicated real fast,
so it's best to have a compatriot,
someone to furnish the pictures
when the inevitable questions come in,
someone you can turn to and say,
"Look, I need a picture of you
in a light blue top and jeans, don't ask,
it's for an experiment."

You will eventually be caught,
or worse, try a new study
to see if whatever they felt for the mask
can transfer to the person under it,
after all they said it was your personality they liked best about
you.
But it wasn't and it won't.

They will say that you lied.
That they fell in love with someone else,
as if no one has ever fallen in love with the mask before,
as if we weren't all taught how to wear these masks in the first
place.

"But he was real gentleman" she said,
"He opened the door for me,
and he bought me dinner."
Those were lies, my dear.
He is just another wolf,
looking for a rabbit.
He learned his lessons well,
that is all.

Those are all just the simple threads
because he bought your drinks too,
and you didn't ask for those.
Such experiments rarely turn out well
for the rabbits.

But I will not use your pictures to catfish,
I will not make you partner to a lie.
I'm sick of the masks anyway,
and the way it itches to wear someone else's skin,
the way their perfectly composed smiles
start showing an awful lot of your own teeth.
And all the compliments you would ever get anyway
do nothing but remind you
that you need to look like someone else,
before you are worth the effort.

What My Light Eye Knows

I lay awake reading on my side
One eye on the page
The other closed against the folds of the pillow
When I got up
The once closed eye was overcompensating
Hungry for light
While the view from the still open eye appeared shrouded now
One eye was dilated more than the other.
My brain had done these adjustments
The body-machine giving no control
Of these functions
To the ghost that lived inside

But the result was a disparity in view
One eye saw life
The dark eye saw death in every shadow
And the ghost inside me started whispering dark secrets

When we die our souls are cut free
Having no mass
Held no more by gravity
With no momentum
Restrained no more by walls
The ghosts inside *are* truly free

But my light eye knows
The earth moves at over 18 miles a second
Spiraling behind a sun that is also moving
Away from the center of all things
And so the course of the earth is a corkscrew shape through the
heavens

My eyes adjust
And these two disparate visions merge
And I see the souls of the dead flying away from us
Or rather they stay still
As the earth rushes away from them
Taking us still living with it

I see now that the earth leaves behind it
A corkscrew comet trail of severed souls
Held no longer to this world
They stretch back behind it
There a single death
There a cluster
Bright spots of souls
Where gas chambers used to be
Pin pricks of light
Seen by my new eyes receding into the past
As the earth moves on
Without them